Contents

Any Ants?

1 ant

2 ants

ants in
my pants

Listen for the Sound

Color the pictures that begin like ant.

Aa

Reading • EMC 4528 • ©2005 by Evan-Moor Corp.

What Does It Say?

Match the word to the picture.

ant

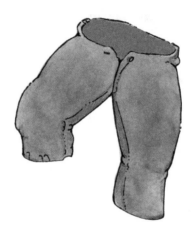

plant

pants

Aa

How Many?

Cut and glue to tell how many.

1 ant

2 ants

3 ants

4 ants

5 ants

6 ants

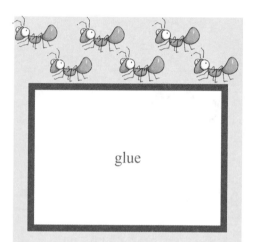

glue

glue

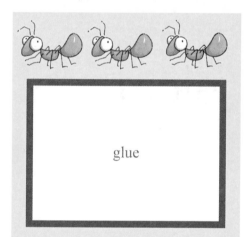

glue

glue

glue

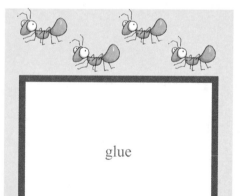

glue

Reading • EMC 4528 • ©2005 by Evan-Moor Corp.

Draw It!

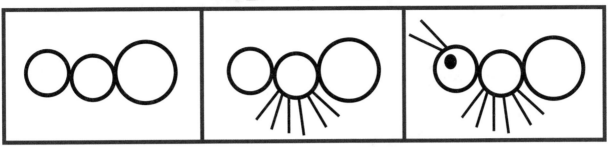

1. Draw 1 red ant.

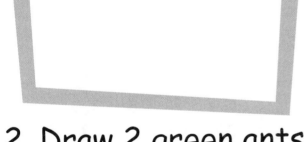

2. Draw 2 green ants.

3. Draw ants on the pants.

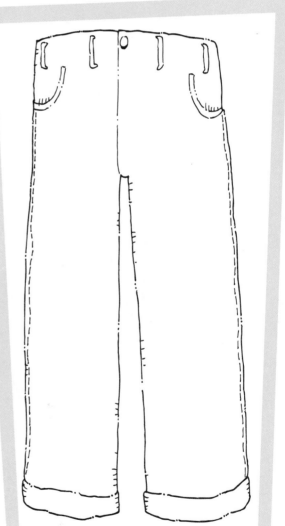

(Aa)

Bouncing Balls

big ball   little ball

See the balls.

Reading • EMC 4528 • ©2005 by Evan-Moor Corp.

Listen for the Sound

Color the pictures that begin with the same sound as ball.

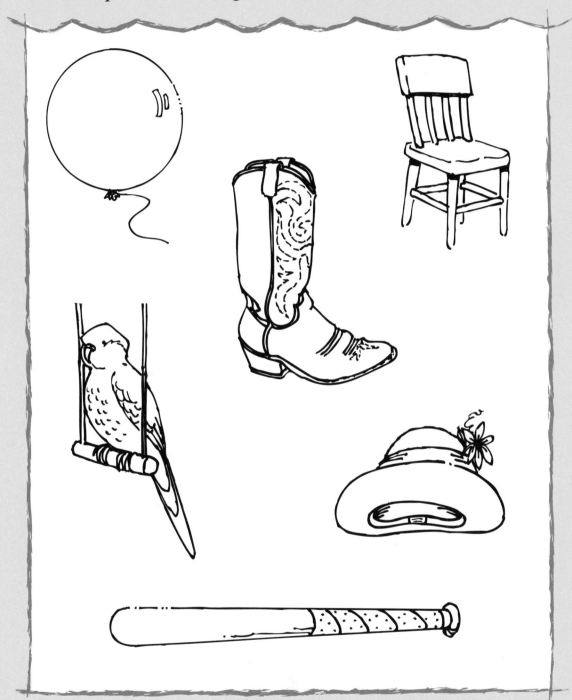

Bb

What Does It Say?

Cut and glue to name each picture. Color the pictures.

box

bed

bat

ball

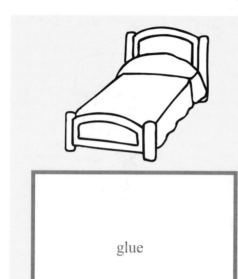

glue

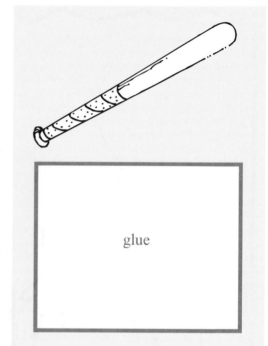

glue

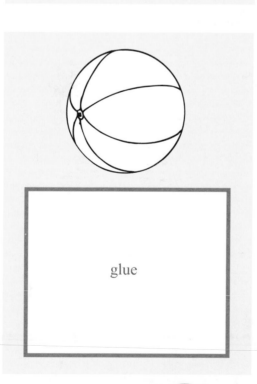

glue

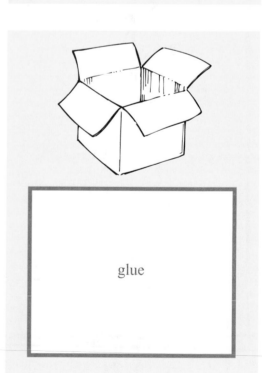

glue

Bb

Big or Little?

Draw 3 **big** things here.

Draw 3 **little** things here.

Seeing Shapes

Color the ◯ ▬▬▬▬ .
Color the △ ▬▬▬▬ .
Color the ▢ ▬▬▬▬ .

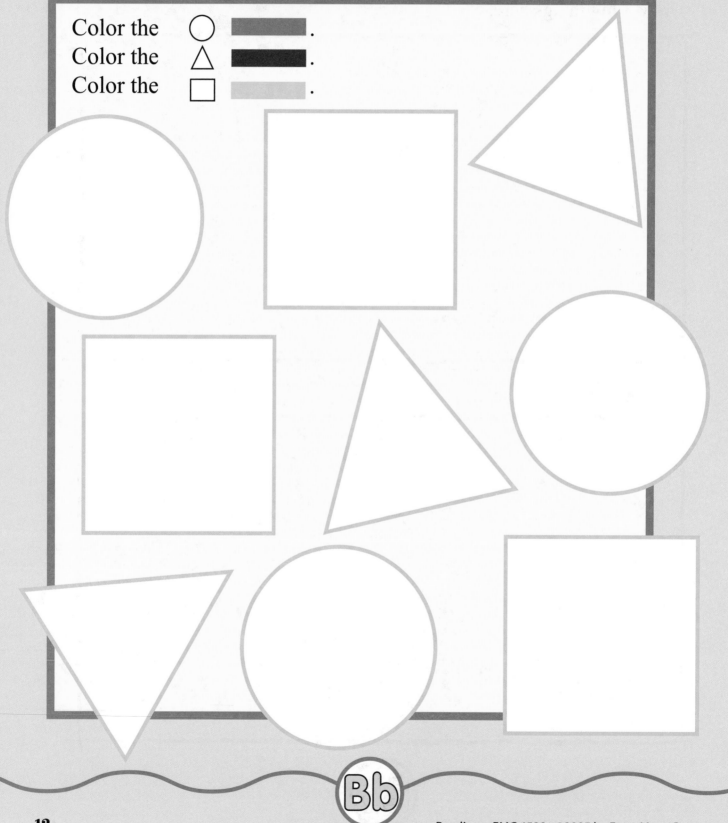

Bb

Reading • EMC 4528 • ©2005 by Evan-Moor Corp.

What Color Is It?

a red car

It's red.

a blue cup

It's blue.

a green cap

It's green.

a yellow cat

It's yellow.

What Does It Say?

Draw a picture to show what the word says.

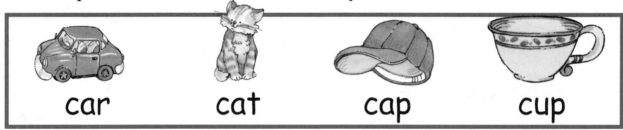

| car | cat | cap | cup |

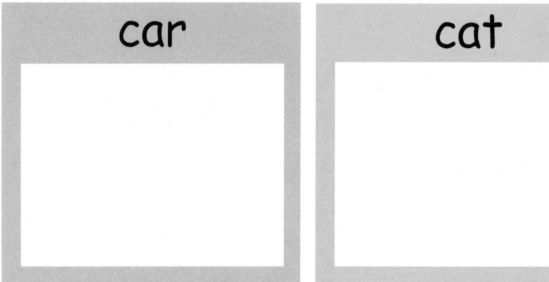

car

cat

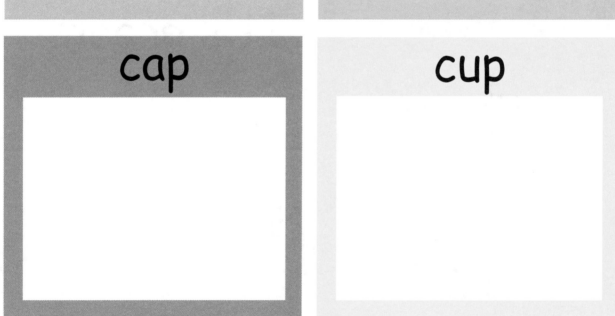

cap

cup

Cc

Listen for the Sound

Cut and glue the pictures that begin with the same sound as car.

glue

glue

glue

glue

glue

Cc

Color the Cat

Trace and write.

cat cat

Cc

Reading • EMC 4528 • ©2005 by Evan-Moor Corp.

In the Cage

Connect the dots to finish the cage. Start with 1.

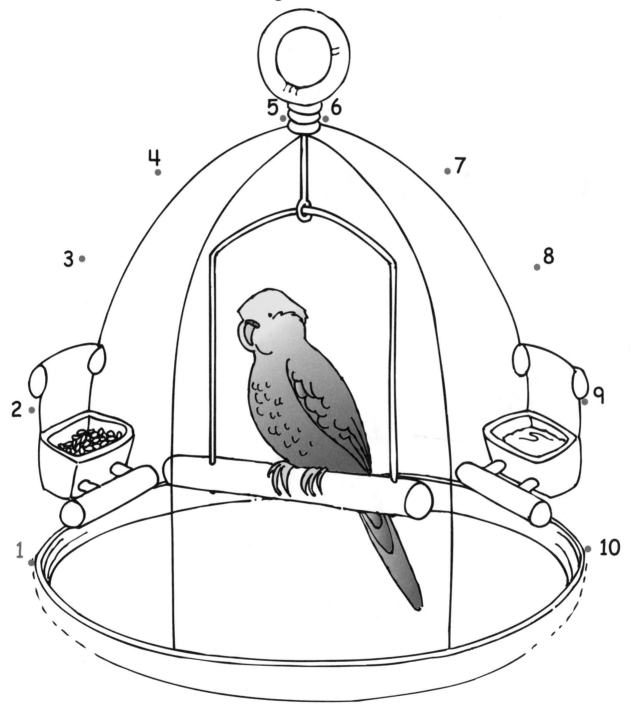

Cc

Digging

Dig, Dog, dig.

Dig, Dog, dig.

After You Read

Practice the story.
Read it to an adult.

Dd

Reading • EMC 4528 • ©2005 by Evan-Moor Corp.

Listen for the Sound

Color the pictures that begin with the same sound as dog.

Dd

What Does It Say?

Draw a line from each name to the correct animal.

dog

cat

mouse

horse

frog

Dd

Reading • EMC 4528 • ©2005 by Evan-Moor Corp.

Dudley Duck

Trace the – – – – lines. Color the picture.

Trace and write.

duck   duck

Dd

A Good Place to Dig

Fill in ◯ yes or ◯ no.

This is a good place to dig.
◯ yes   ◯ no

This is a good place to dig.
◯ yes   ◯ no

This is a good place to dig.
◯ yes   ◯ no

This is a good place to dig.
◯ yes   ◯ no

Dd

Eggs

big eggs

little eggs

pretty eggs

Ee

Listen for the Sound

Color the pictures that begin with the same sound as egg.
Make an **X** on the pictures that begin with a different sound.

Ee

Reading • EMC 4528 • ©2005 by Evan-Moor Corp.

Seeing Words

Circle the words that are the same as the first word in each row.

egg	egg	eagle	egg
big	dig	big	big
little	little	little	lift
candy	dandy	candy	candy
good	good	dog	good

Ee

What Does It Say?

Circle the word that names the picture.

	ball	rug
	pen	cat
	egg	leg
	book	ant
	dog	moon
	sun	cap

Ee

Reading • EMC 4528 • ©2005 by Evan-Moor Corp.

Is It Real?

Fill in ◯ yes or ◯ no.

Is it real?
◯ **yes**   ◯ **no**

Is it real?
◯ **yes**   ◯ **no**

Is it real?
◯ **yes**   ◯ **no**

Is it real?
◯ **yes**   ◯ **no**

Swim, Fish, Swim

Little fish, little fish,
Swish, swish, swish.

Listen for the Sound

Cut and glue to show which pictures
begin with the same sound as fish.

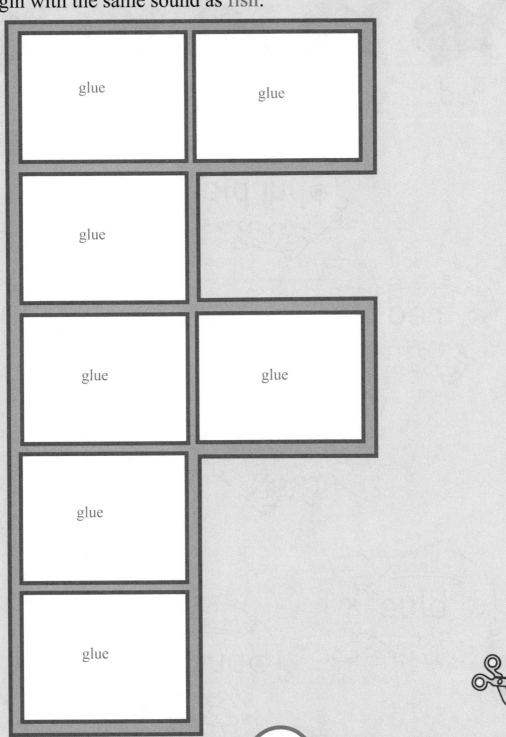

Ff

What Does It Say?

Color the fish.

red   green   blue   purple   yellow

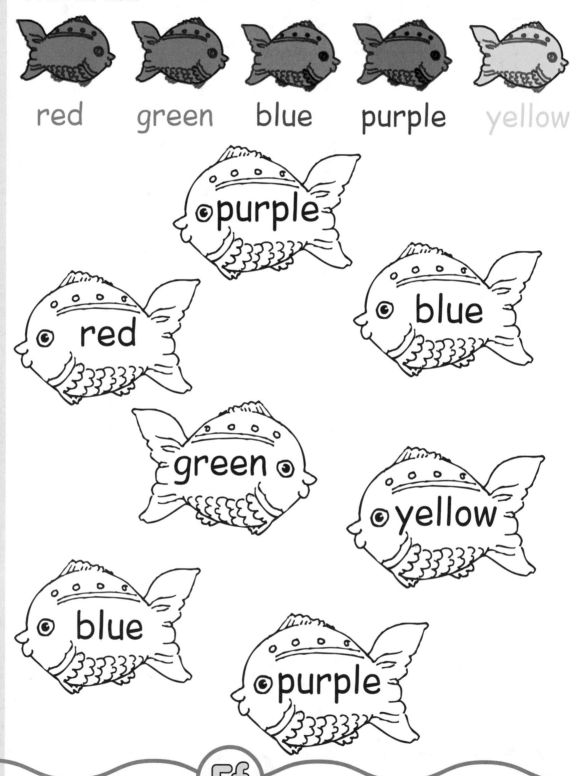

Ff

Rhyme Time

Circle the pictures in each line that rhyme.

Ff

How Many?

Count. Write the number to tell how many.

———   ———   ———

———   ———   ———

Ff

Good and Bad

Good!

Bad!

Good!

Bad!

What a day I had!

Gg

Listen for the Sound

Color the pictures that begin with the same sound as goat.

Gg

Put It in Order

Color, cut, and glue. Put the pictures in order.

1

glue

2

glue

3

glue

4

glue

Gg

G at the End

Circle the pictures that have the same ending sound as bag.

Gg

Reading • EMC 4528 • ©2005 by Evan-Moor Corp.

What Do You Think?

Trace.

Write good or bad.

Gg

Hippo's Hat

one hat
one big hat
one big red hat

Hh

Listen for the Sound

Circle the pictures that begin with the same sound as hippo.

Hh

39

What Does It Say?

Draw a picture to show what each word means.

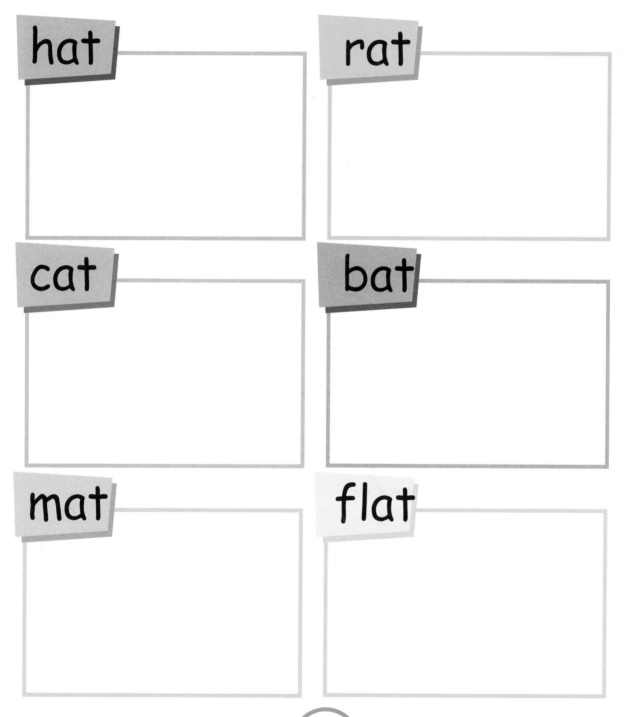

hat

rat

cat

bat

mat

flat

Hh

The House on the Hill

Follow the dots to make a hill.
Color the hill.
Draw a house on top.

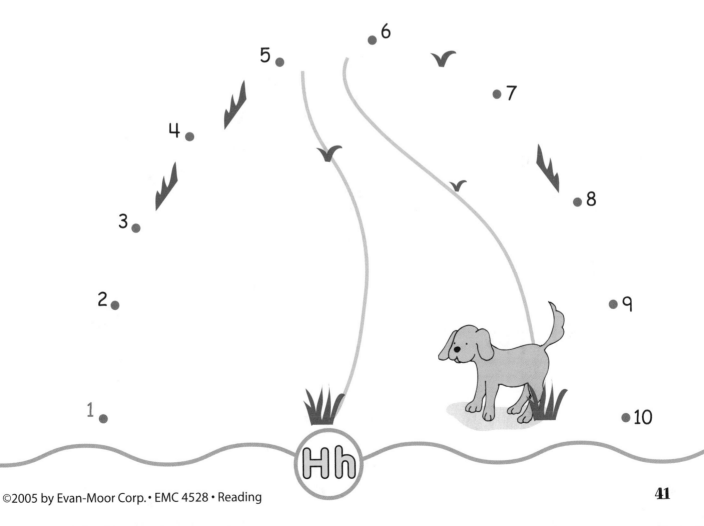

Hh

©2005 by Evan-Moor Corp. • EMC 4528 • Reading

41

Is He Happy?

Fill in ◯ yes or ◯ no.

Is he happy?  ◯ yes
◯ no

Is he happy?  ◯ yes
◯ no

Is he happy?  ◯ yes
◯ no

Is he happy?  ◯ yes
◯ no

Hh

What's Inside?

Lift the lid.
See what hid.

in a box

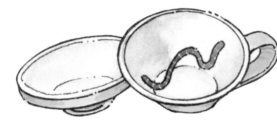 in a cup

in a jar

Close it up!

Ii

What Can You Do?

Read the words. Draw a picture to show what they say.

I can stop.

I can go.

Reading • EMC 4528 • ©2005 by Evan-Moor Corp.

Skills: Categorizing; Using Scissors

Interesting Insects!

Color, cut, and glue. Put the insects in the jar.

My Insect Zoo

glue   glue

glue   glue

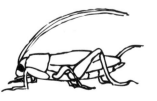

Ii

In or Out?

Where is it? Fill in ◯ **in** or ◯ **out**.

◯ in

◯ out

◯ in

◯ out

◯ in

◯ out

◯ in

◯ out

◯ in

◯ out

◯ in

◯ out

Reading • EMC 4528 • ©2005 by Evan-Moor Corp.

Find the Words

Circle the words that are the same in each row.

big	big	dig	big
pig	dig	pig	pig
wig	wig	wig	mig
kick	lick	kick	kick
sick	sick	slick	sick
hill	hall	hill	hill

Ii

Just a Jar

What's in the jar?

jam

What's in the jar?

jelly beans

What's in the jar?

June bug

After You Read

Practice the story.

Make it sound like you are asking questions.

Read it to an adult.

Jj

Reading • EMC 4528 • ©2005 by Evan-Moor Corp.

Listen for the Sound

Cut and glue the pictures that begin with the same sound as jar.

glue

glue

glue

glue

glue

What Does It Say?

Match each word to a picture. Color the pictures.

jar

jam

jet

jeep

Jj

How Many Balls?

Color. Count. Write the number word to tell how many.

_____ balls

_____ balls

_____ balls

_____ ball

Word Box

| one | two | three | four | five | six |

Just Jack

Color each puzzle piece that has a dot.

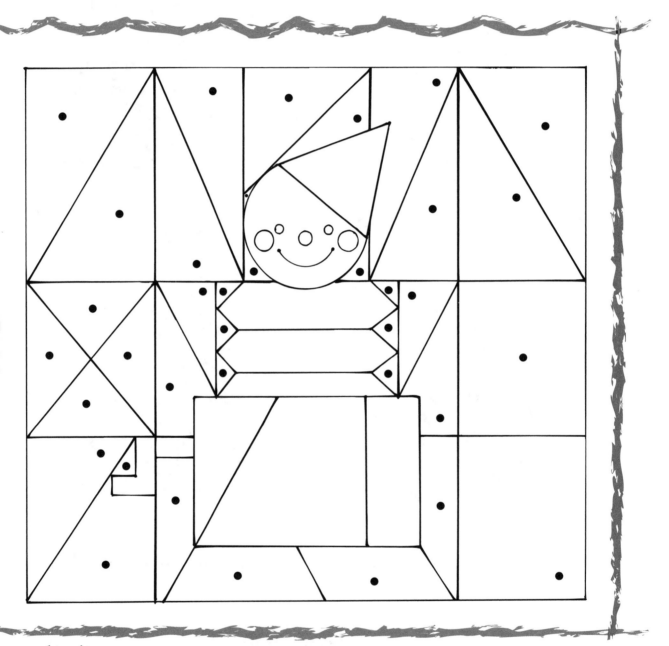

Trace and write.

See Jack.

Important Keys

Lock it up!

a key for the suitcase

Lock it up!

a key for the door

Start it up!

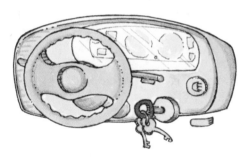

a key for the car

Here we go!

Kk

Listen for the Sound

Circle the pictures that begin with the same sound as key.

Kk

Reading • EMC 4528 • ©2005 by Evan-Moor Corp.

Kites, Kites, Kites

Read the color words. Color the kites.

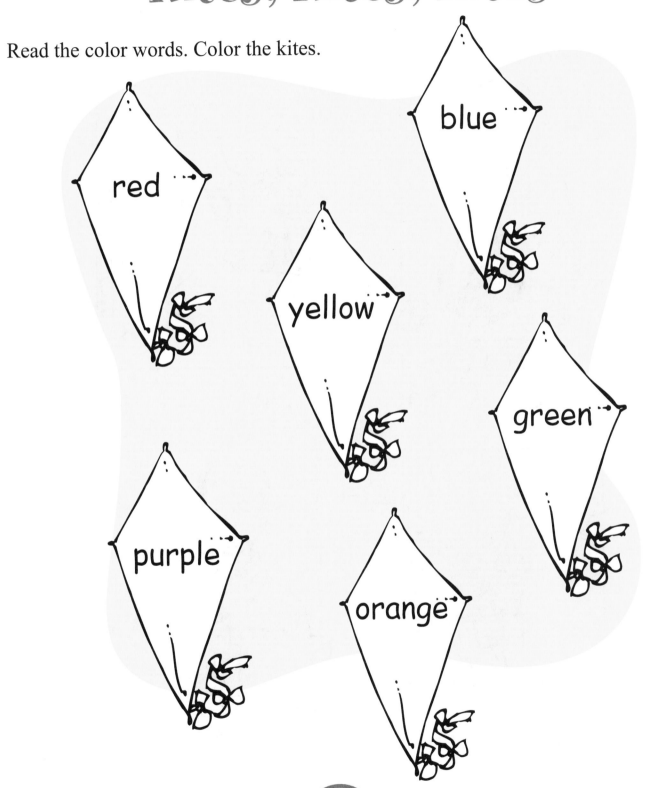

red

blue

yellow

green

purple

orange

Kk

Kindergarten

Could it happen in kindergarten? Fill in ◯ yes ◯ or no.

◯ yes ◯ no

◯ yes ◯ no

◯ yes ◯ no

◯ yes ◯ no

Kk

New Words

The pictures show what each new **k** word means. Draw a line to show who would use each thing.

kennel

kerchief

kettle

kayak

Kk

Let's Go to the Zoo

Look!

a lion

a llama

a leopard

a lollipop

Ll

Reading • EMC 4528 • ©2005 by Evan-Moor Corp.

Listen for the Sound

Say the name of each picture. Do you hear the **l** sound first or last?

Fill in ⭕ first or ⭕ last.

⭕ first ⭕ last   ⭕ first ⭕ last   ⭕ first ⭕ last

⭕ first ⭕ last   ⭕ first ⭕ last   ⭕ first ⭕ last

⭕ first ⭕ last   ⭕ first ⭕ last   ⭕ first ⭕ last

Ll

Little or Large?

Color the pictures. Make an **X** on the little one.

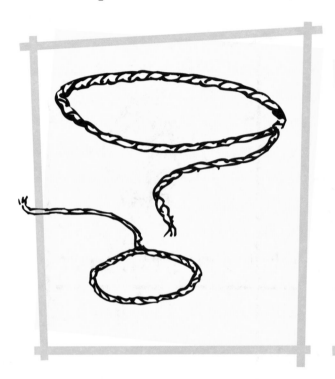

Ll

Look!
I can make new words!

Start with look.   l o o k

Take off the l.
Write a b.   ___ o o k

Take off the b.
Write an h.   ___ o o k

Take off the h.
Write a c   ___ o o k

Take off the c.
Write br.   ___ ___ o o k

L l

What's for Lunch?

Color the pictures that show food.

LI

Special Places

Little mouse
has a house.

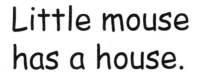

Little mole
has a hole.

Little me
in a tepee.

Mm

Listen for the Sound

Color the pictures that begin with the same sound as mouse.

Mm

Reading • EMC 4528 • ©2005 by Evan-Moor Corp.

Match the Mittens

Cut and glue to make pairs.

glue	glue

glue	glue

Mm

Where Am I?

Draw a line to make a match.

Find my house.

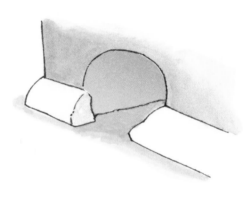

Find my tepee.

Find my hole.

Mm

Reading • EMC 4528 • ©2005 by Evan-Moor Corp.

In the Night Sky

Connect the dots. Start with **1**. Color the picture.

.3

4.

.2

5.

.20

.19

.1

. 18

6 .

6

. 17

13 .

7 .

. 16

14 .   .12

.15

8

11

9

10

Have you ever seen the moon?

○ yes   ○ no

Mm

The New One

Is it in the nest?

No

Is it in the net?

No

It's in the nursery!

Yes!

Listen for the Sound

Cut and glue the pictures that begin with the same sound as net.

glue

glue

glue

glue

glue

Nn

No, No, No

Write yes or no.

 The ball is red. _____

 The ball is green. _____

 The ball is yellow. _____

 The ball is brown. _____

Do you have a ball? _____

Do you play with a ball? _____

Nn

Noodle Necklace

Cut and glue. Make a necklace.

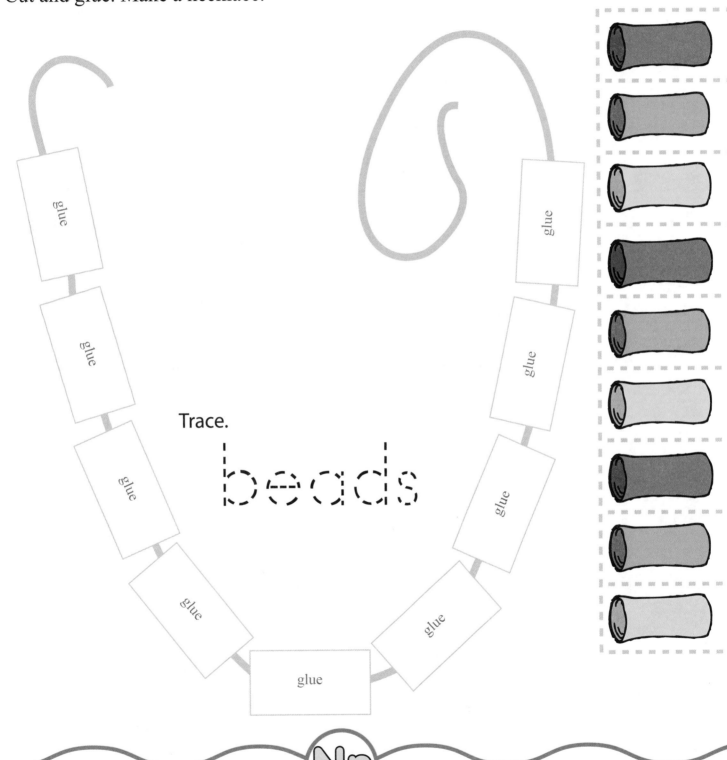

glue

glue

glue

glue

glue

glue

glue

glue

glue

Trace.

beads

Nn

Naughty or Nice?

Circle the word to tell whether they are naughty or nice.

○ naughty ○ nice

○ naughty ○ nice

○ naughty ○ nice

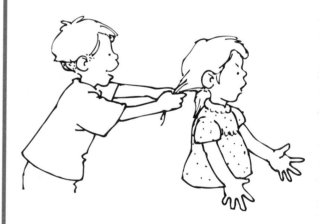

○ naughty ○ nice

Reading • EMC 4528 • ©2005 by Evan-Moor Corp.

Where Do They Live?

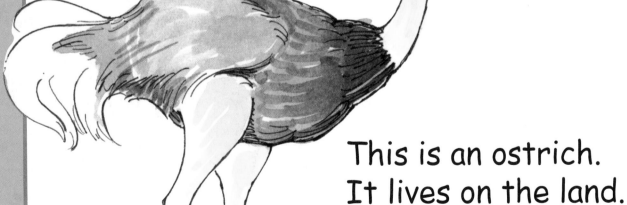

This is an otter.
It lives in the water.

This is an ostrich.
It lives on the land.

O o

Listen for the Sound

Color the pictures that begin with the same sound as otter.

Reading • EMC 4528 • ©2005 by Evan-Moor Corp.

Making New Words

Add a letter to –and to make a new word that tells what the picture is.

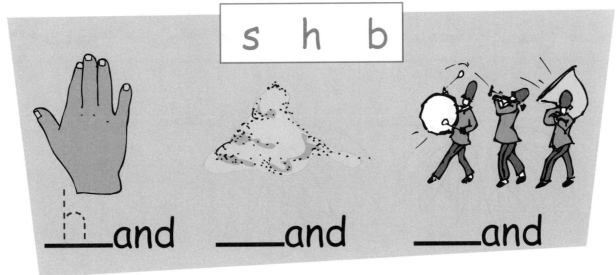

s h b

___and ___and ___and

Write one of the new words in each sentence.

Dump the ___sand___.

Wash your _____.

Hear the _____.

Make Them Look the Same

Look at the first picture. Draw to make the pictures next to it look the same.

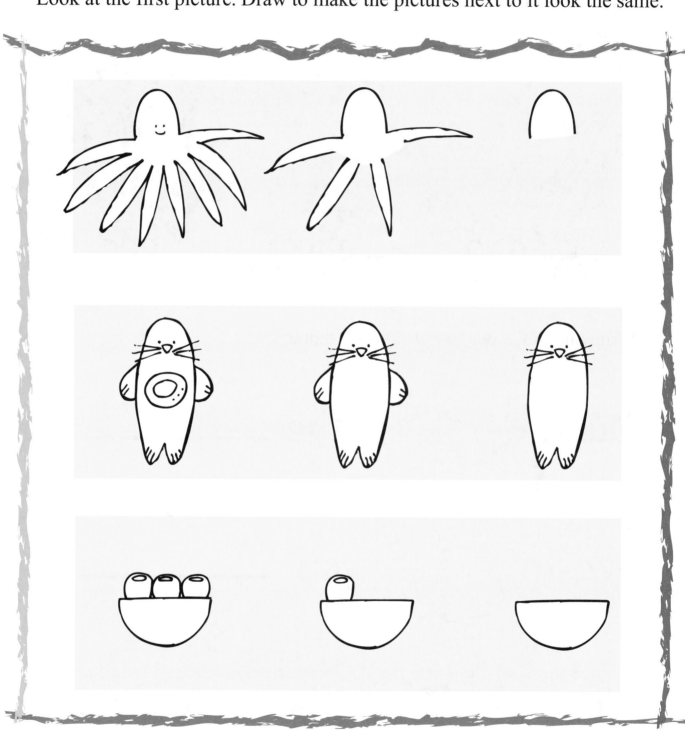

Rhyme Time

Circle the pictures that rhyme with frog.

 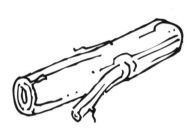 

Circle the pictures that rhyme with rock.

Circle the pictures that rhyme with top.

In a Puddle

The puppy's in a puddle.

The pig's in a puddle.

I'm in a puddle, too.

Listen for the Sound

Color the pictures that begin with the
same sound as pig.

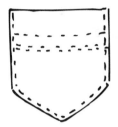

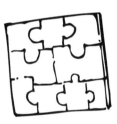

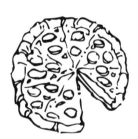

Pp

What Does It Say?

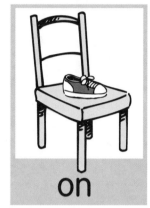  

on   by   under

Read the sentence. Circle the correct picture.

The is on the pot.

The  is by the pot.

The  is under the pot.

Pp

In the Pen

Draw: one pink pig
two black sheep
three yellow chicks

Puzzles, Puzzles, Puzzles

Put the puzzles together. Fill in ⃝ yes or ⃝ no.

Do you like pickles?

⃝ yes   ⃝ no

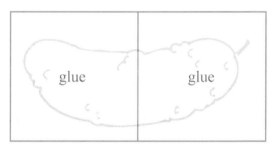

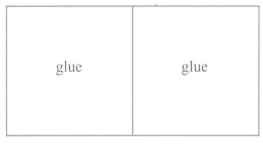

Do you like popcorn?

⃝ yes   ⃝ no

Do you like pancakes?

⃝ yes   ⃝ no

Do you like pizza?

⃝ yes   ⃝ no

Pp

Reading • EMC 4528 • ©2005 by Evan-Moor Corp.

Quack, quack, quack.

Be quiet!

Quack, quack, quack.

Be quiet!

Quack, quack, quack.

Quiet!

Qq

Listen for the Sound

Color the pictures that begin with the same sound as quack.

Quack

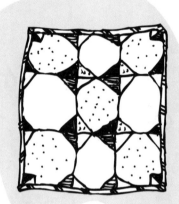

Qq

What Does It Say?

Match each word to a picture. Draw a line.

duck

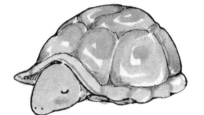

frog

turtle

alligator

Yes or No?

Fill in ◯ yes or ◯ no.

1. A  says "Quack."

◯ yes ◯ no

2. An  says "Quack."

◯ yes ◯ no

3. A  says "Quack."

◯ yes ◯ no

4. A  says "Quack."

◯ yes ◯ no

Qq

Reading • EMC 4528 • ©2005 by Evan-Moor Corp.

Seeing Words

Circle the words that are the same as the first word in each row.

jump	jump	run	jump
sleep	slip	sleep	sleep
quack	quack	quack	quiet
sit	sip	sit	sit
dog	dog	bog	dog
home	home	house	home

Qq

The Race

Run, rabbit, run.

Run, rooster, run.

Run, rhinoceros, run.

What a race!

Rr

Reading • EMC 4528 • ©2005 by Evan-Moor Corp.

Listen for the Sound

Cut and glue the pictures that begin with the same sound as rabbit.

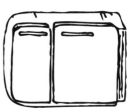

glue

glue

glue

glue

glue

glue

Rr

What Does It Say?

Draw a line from each sentence to the correct picture.

I can run.

I can rest.

I can read.

Rr

Reading • EMC 4528 • ©2005 by Evan-Moor Corp.

Draw It!

Follow the pictures to draw a robot. Give the robot a name.

Find the Rhyme

Circle the pictures in each row that rhyme.

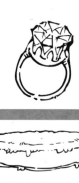  

Rr

Reading • EMC 4528 • ©2005 by Evan-Moor Corp.

Sad Sam

See Sam.
Sam is sad.

See Sam.
Sam is so sad.
Sad, sad Sam.

After You Read

Practice the story.
Make it sound sad.
Read it to an adult.

Listen for the Sound 6

Color the pictures that begin with the same sound as six.

Ss

Reading • EMC 4528 • ©2005 by Evan-Moor Corp.

What Does It Say?

Circle the word that tells about the picture. Write the word in the sentence.

sad   glad

Sam is _____.

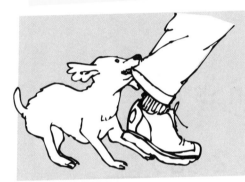

mad   sad

The dog is _____.

Bad   Dad

_____ kitty!

sad   glad

Sam is _____.

Ss

More Than One

Add **s** to the end of the word to mean more than one. Color the pictures.

1 sock

3 sock_s__

1 sub

2 sub____

1 star

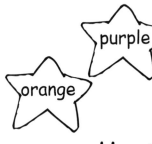

4 star____

1 spoon

2 spoon___

Ss

Reading • EMC 4528 • ©2005 by Evan-Moor Corp.

Dot-to-Dot

Connect the dots. Start with 1.

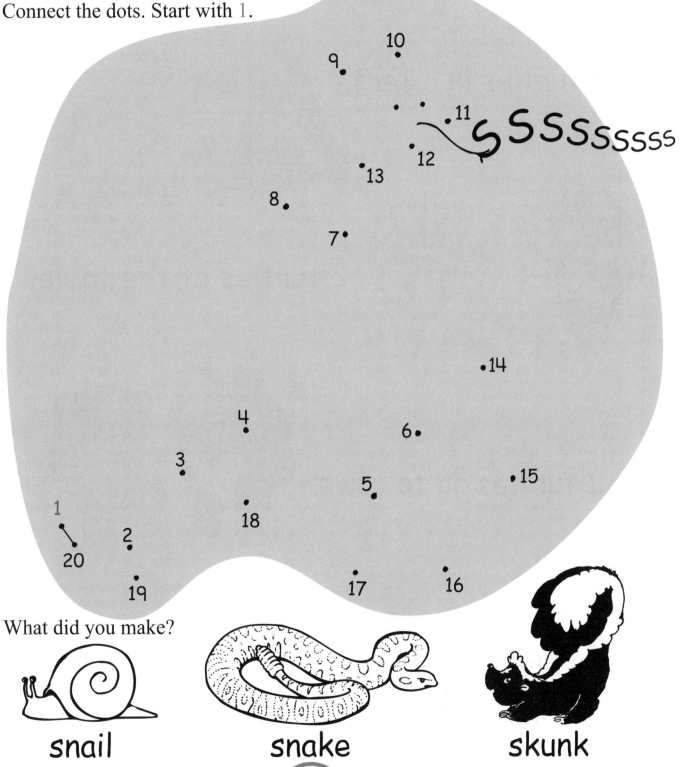

What did you make?

snail

snake

skunk

Ss

On the Trail

2 turtles in a tent.

2 turtles at the table.

2 turtles go to town.

2 tired turtles!

Tt

Reading • EMC 4528 • ©2005 by Evan-Moor Corp.

Listen for the Sound

Cut and glue the pictures that begin with the same sound as tent.

glue	glue	glue

glue

glue

glue

glue

glue

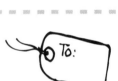

Tt

First or Last?

Say the name of each picture. Circle first or last to tell where you hear the **t** sound.

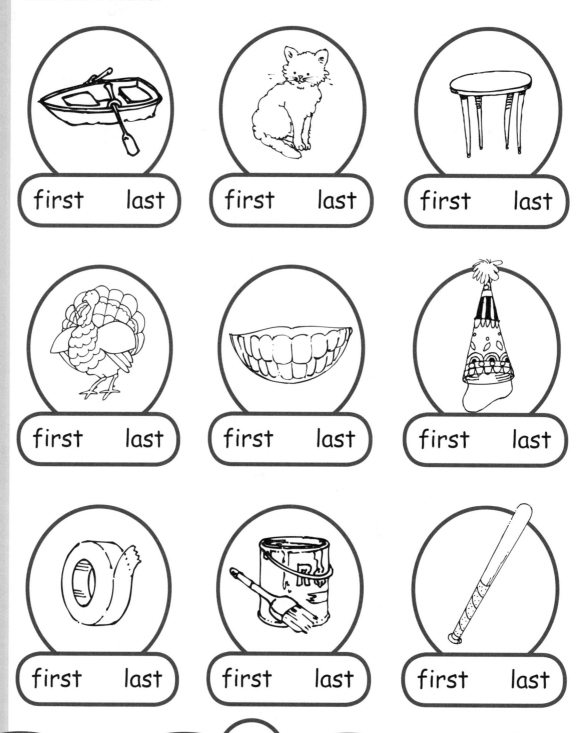

first   last

first   last

first   last

first   last

first   last

first   last

first   last

first   last

first   last

What Does It Say?

Look at each picture. Write the first letter and the last letter of each word.

Circle the animals that have 4 legs.

What Will Come Next?

Circle the picture that shows what will happen next.

 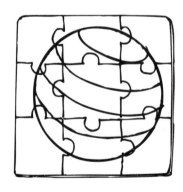 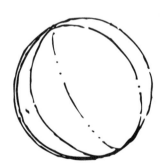

Up, up, up, up, up, up.

Down!

Uu

Listen for the Sound

Color the pictures that begin with the same sound as umbrella.

Uu

Up or Down?

Write up or down.

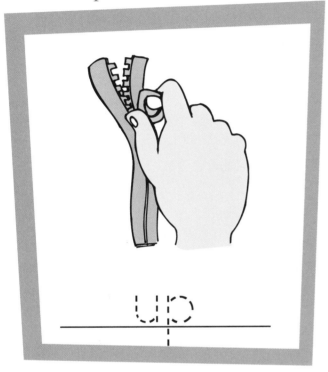

up

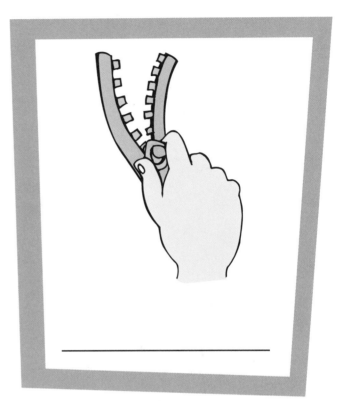

Uu

Who Is Under the Umbrella?

Draw a line to show who is under each umbrella.

Reading • EMC 4528 • ©2005 by Evan-Moor Corp.

Read and Color

Read the words. Color the umbrella.

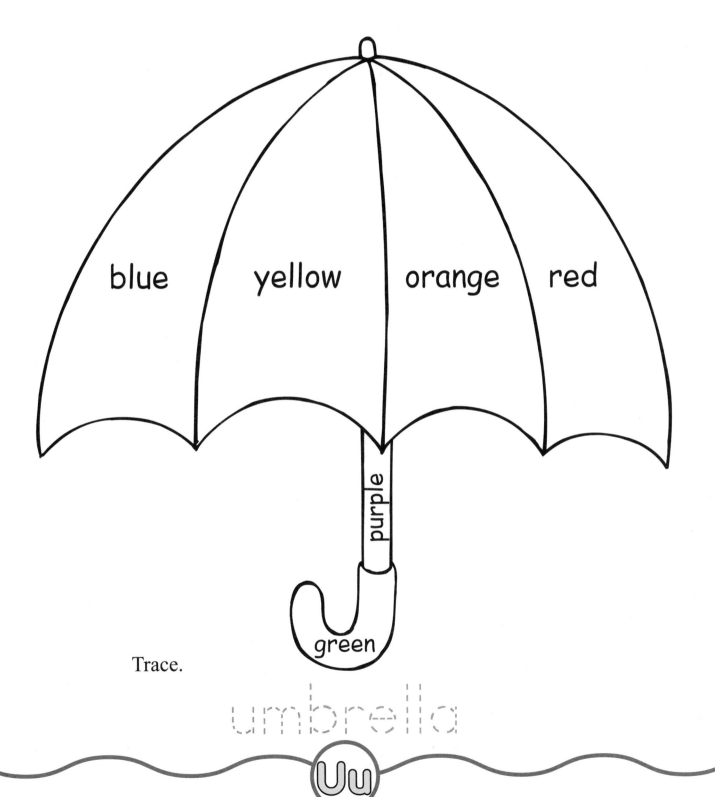

blue   yellow   orange   red

purple

green

Trace.

umbrella

Uu

Very Nice!

See my vest.
It's the best.

Very nice.

See my van.
It is tan.

Very nice.

See my vine.
It's just fine.

Very nice.

Vv

Listen for the Sound

Cut and glue the pictures that begin with the same sound as vine.

glue	glue
glue	glue
glue	glue

Vv

In the Garden

Color the vegetables.
Circle the vegetable you like the very best.

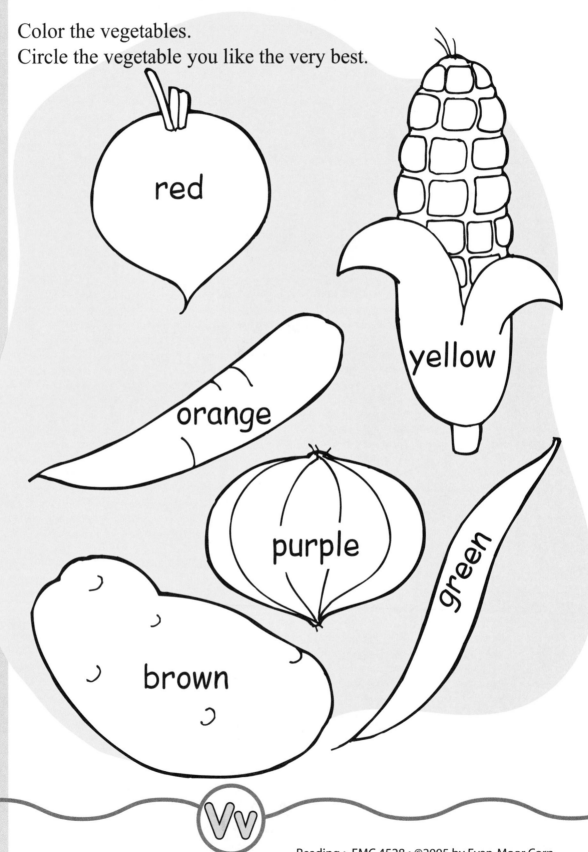

red

yellow

orange

purple

green

brown

Vv

What Does It Say?

Draw a line to match each word to a picture.

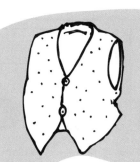

cave

vest

hive

stove

Vv

Draw It!

Follow the pictures to draw a van. Color the van.

Reading • EMC 4528 • ©2005 by Evan-Moor Corp.

Waffle Wagon

What's in the wagon?

weeds

What's in the wagon?

water

What's in the wagon?

wood

What's in the wagon?

Ww

Listen for the Sound

Color the pictures that begin with the same sound as wagon.

Waffles!

Ww

Reading • EMC 4528 • ©2005 by Evan-Moor Corp.

What Does It Say?

Look at each picture.
Draw what you
should do.

Walk

Wait

Seeing Words

Circle the words in each row that are the same as the first word.

| with | with | will | with | with |

| went | won | went | went | went |

| was | was | was | saw | was |

| what | when | what | what | what |

| wish | wish | wish | wash | wish |

| wag | wag | wag | nag | wag |

Ww

Make a Wish

Follow the dots. Start with 1.

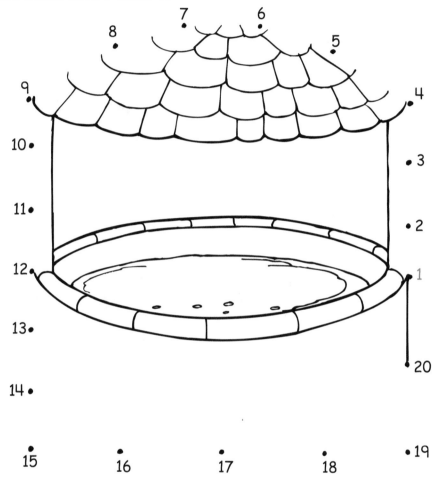

Have you made a wish at a wishing well?

◯ yes   ◯ no

What did you wish for?

_____

Take an X-ray.

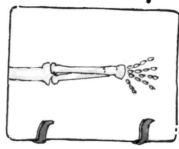  

Exit here.

Take an X-ray.

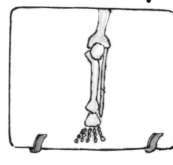 

Exit here.

Take an X-ray.

Exit here.

Xx

Reading • EMC 4528 • ©2005 by Evan-Moor Corp.

Listen for the Sound

Color the pictures that have the same ending sound as fox.
Write the end letter of each word.

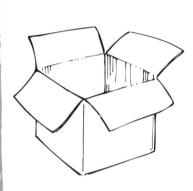

bo x

a __

ca __

o __

si __

do __

Xx

What Does It Say?

Color the spaces with dots. Read the sign.

Follow the Directions

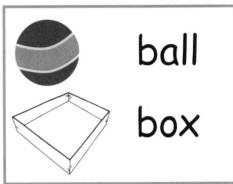

ball

box

See the box.

Draw 3 balls in the box.

Color the balls blue.

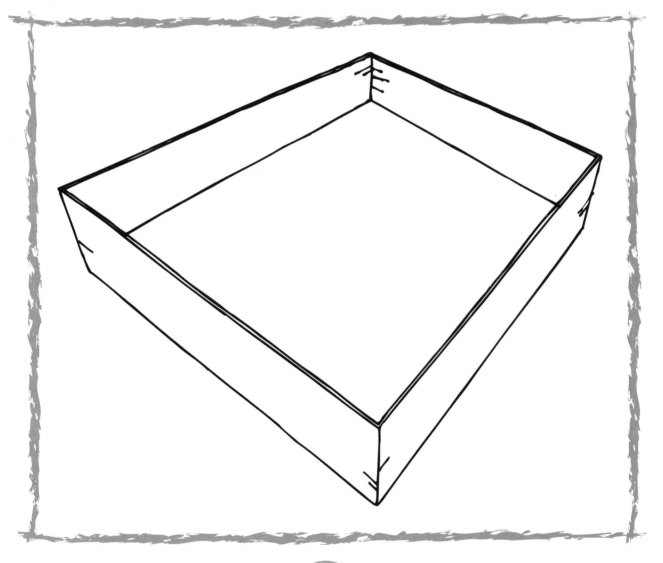

Rhyme Time

Circle the pictures that rhyme.

Time to Eat

Yum!

Yum!

Yuck!

After You Read

Practice the story.
Make it sound funny.
Read it to an adult.

Yy

Answer the Questions

Answer the questions. Write **yes** or **no**.

Do you like  ? _____

Do you like  ? _____

Do you like  ? _____

Do you like  ? _____

Do you like  ? _____

Do you like  ? _____

Yy

Reading • EMC 4528 • ©2005 by Evan-Moor Corp.

Listen for the Sound

Cut and glue the pictures that begin with the same sound as yum.

glue

glue

glue

glue

glue

glue

Yy

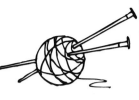

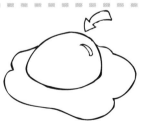

The -um Family

Write each word. Draw a line to the picture that matches.
Color the pictures.

g + um = _____gum_____

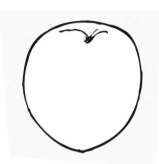

dr + um = _____

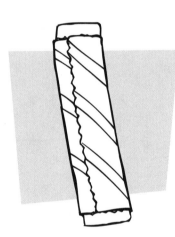

pl + um = _____

Yy

What Did Grandma Make?

Grandma made me a present. She made it out of yarn.
Color the shapes.

red = circles

blue = triangles

yellow = rectangles

Beyond Zero

How many  ?

0   1   2

How many  ?

0   1   2

How many  ?

0   1   2
Zillions!

Reading • EMC 4528 • ©2005 by Evan-Moor Corp.

Listen for the Sound

Color the pictures that begin with the same sound as zipper.

Zz

Seeing Words

Circle the words in each row that are the same as the first word.

| zip | zap | zip | zip | zip |

| zonk | zonk | honk | zonk | zonk |

| zany | zany | sany | zany | zany |

| zing | zing | zing | sing | zing |

| zap | lap | zap | zap | zap |

Zz

Reading • EMC 4528 • ©2005 by Evan-Moor Corp.

Tracking Form

Topic	Color in each page you complete.			
Unit 1 Letter A	4	5	6	7
Unit 2 Letter B	9	10	11	12
Unit 3 Letter C	14	15	16	17
Unit 4 Letter D	19	20	21	22
Unit 5 Letter E	24	25	26	27
Unit 6 Letter F	29	30	31	32
Unit 7 Letter G	34	35	36	37
Unit 8 Letter H	39	40	41	42
Unit 9 Letter I	44	45	46	47
Unit 10 Letter J	49	50	51	52
Unit 11 Letter K	54	55	56	57
Unit 12 Letter L	59	60	61	62
Unit 13 Letter M	64	65	66	67
Unit 14 Letter N	69	70	71	72
Unit 15 Letter O	74	75	76	77
Unit 16 Letter P	79	80	81	82
Unit 17 Letter Q	84	85	86	87
Unit 18 Letter R	89	90	91	92
Unit 19 Letter S	94	95	96	97
Unit 20 Letter T	99	100	101	102

Tracking Form

Topic	Color in each page you complete.			
Unit 21 Letter U	104	105	106	107
Unit 22 Letter V	109	110	111	112
Unit 23 Letter W	114	115	116	117
Unit 24 Letter X	119	120	121	122
Unit 25 Letter Y	124	125	126	127
Unit 26 Letter Z	129	130		

Answer Key

Page 4

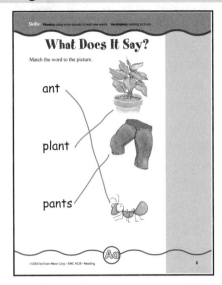

Page 5

Page 6

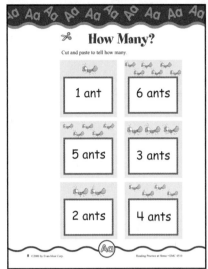

Page 7

Page 9

Page 10

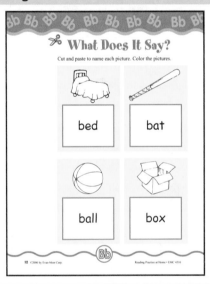

Page 11

Page 12

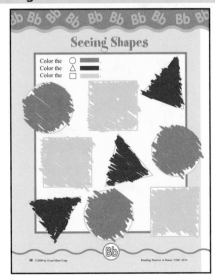

Page 14

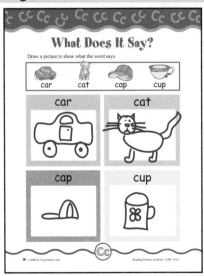

Page 15

Listen for the Sound

Cut and paste the pictures that begin with the same sound as car.

Page 16

Color the Cat

Trace and write.

cat cat

Page 17

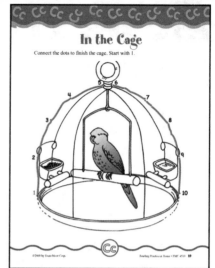

In the Cage

Connect the dots to finish the cage. Start with 1.

Page 19

Listen for the Sound

Color the pictures that begin with the same sound as dog.

donut
dog dish
door
duck
dinosaur
dime

Page 20

What Does It Say?

Draw a line to the right animal.

dog
cat
mouse
horse
frog

Page 21

Dudley Duck

Trace the – – – – lines. Color the picture.

Page 22

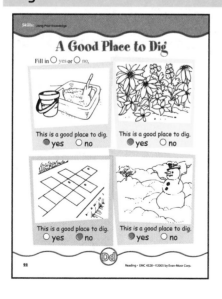

A Good Place to Dig

Fill in ○ yes or ○ no.

This is a good place to dig.
● yes   ○ no

This is a good place to dig.
● yes   ○ no

This is a good place to dig.
○ yes   ● no

This is a good place to dig.
○ yes   ● no

Page 24

Listen for the Sound

Color the pictures that begin with the same sound as egg.
Make an X on the pictures that begin with a different sound.

exit
elevator
escalator
envelope
elbow
elephant

Page 25

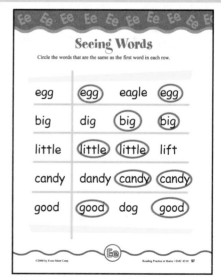

Seeing Words

Circle the words that are the same as the first word in each row.

egg	egg	eagle	egg
big	dig	big	big
little	little	little	lift
candy	dandy	candy	candy
good	good	dog	good

Reading • EMC 4528 • ©2005 by Evan-Moor Corp.

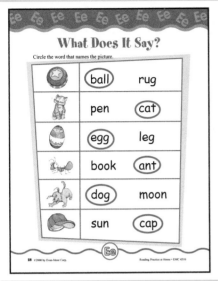

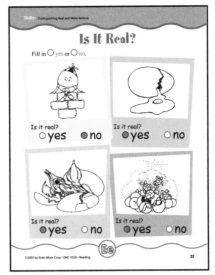

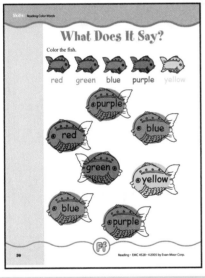

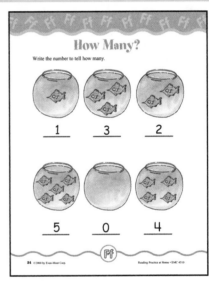

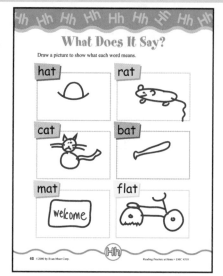

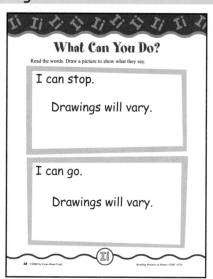

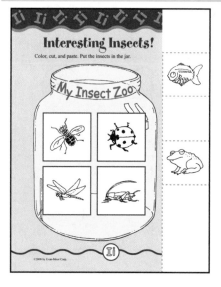

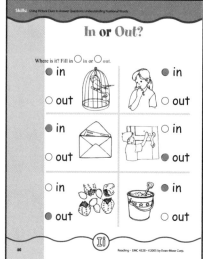

Reading • EMC 4528 • ©2005 by Evan-Moor Corp.

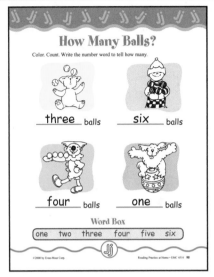

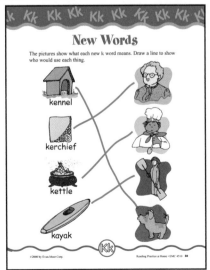

©2005 by Evan-Moor Corp. • EMC 4528 • Reading

Little or Large?

Color the pictures. Put an X on the little one.

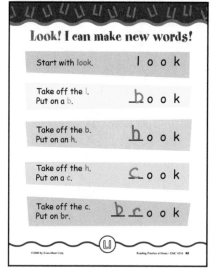

Look! I can make new words!

Start with look.	l o o k
Take off the l. Put on a b.	b o o k
Take off the b. Put on an h.	h o o k
Take off the h. Put on a c.	c o o k
Take off the c. Put on br.	b r o o k

What's for Lunch?

Color the food.

Listen for the Sound

Color the pictures that begin with the same sound as mouse.

mail   mitten   moose   mouse   mitt   monkey   map

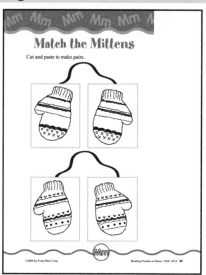

Match the Mittens

Cut and paste to make pairs.

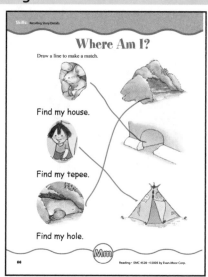

Where Am I?

Draw a line to make a match.

Find my house.

Find my tepee.

Find my hole.

In the Night Sky

Connect the dots. Start with 1. Color the picture.

Have you ever seen the moon?   Answers will vary.

yes   no

Listen for the Sound

Cut and paste to show what pictures begin with the same sound as net.

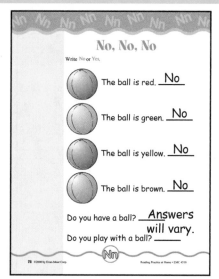

No, No, No

Write No or Yes.

The ball is red. No

The ball is green. No

The ball is yellow. No

The ball is brown. No

Do you have a ball? Answers will vary.

Do you play with a ball? _____

Noodle Necklace

Cut and paste. Make a necklace.

Patterns will vary.

Naughty or Nice?

Circle the word to tell whether they are naughty or nice.

- ● naughty ○ nice
- ○ naughty ● nice
- ○ naughty ● nice
- ● naughty ○ nice

Listen for the Sound

Color the pictures that begin like otter.

otter, ostrich, olive, octopus

Making New Words

Add a letter to -and to make a new word that tells what the picture is.

h and   s and   b and

Write one of the new words in each sentence.

Dump the _sand_.

Wash your _hand_.

Hear the _band_.

Make Them Look the Same

Look at the first thing. Make the others the same.

Rhyme Time

Color the pictures that rhyme with frog.

dog, log

Color the pictures that rhyme with rock.

lock, sock

Color the pictures that rhyme with top.

mop, drop, stop

Listen for the Sound

Color the pictures to show the words that begin with the sound that p stands for.

pocket, potato, pencil, puzzle, popcorn, penny, pizza, pumpkin, pig, paint

What Does It Say?

on   by   under

Read the sentence. Circle the correct picture.

The ___ is on the pot.

The ___ is by the pot.

The ___ is under the pot.

In the Pen

Draw: one pink pig
two black sheep
three yellow chicks

Drawings will vary.
There should be
1 pig, 2 sheep, and
3 chicks.

Page 82

Page 83

Page 85

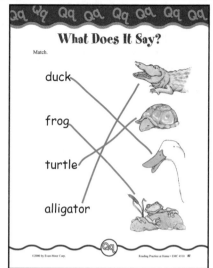

Page 86

Page 87

Page 89

Page 90

Page 91

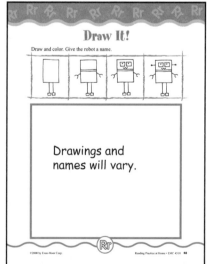

Page 92

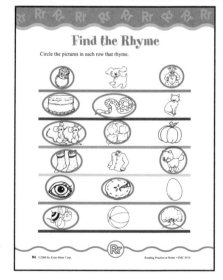

Page 94

Page 95

Page 96

Page 97

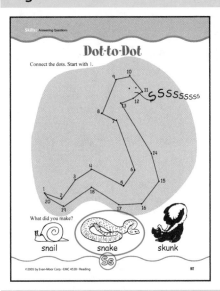

Page 99

Page 100

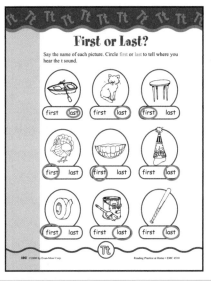

Page 101

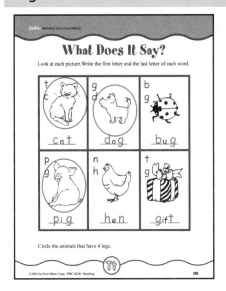

Page 102

Page 104

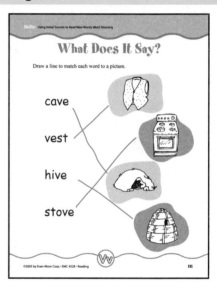

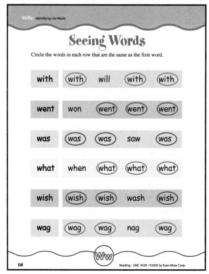

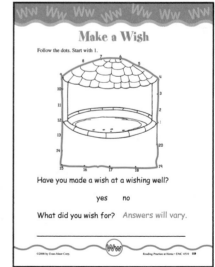

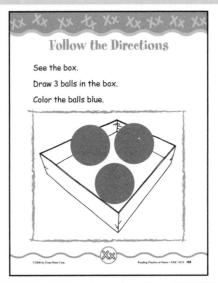

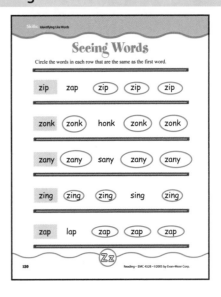